Full STEAM Ahead!
Science Starters

The Right Material for the Job

Crystal Sikkens

CRABTREE
PUBLISHING COMPANY
WWW.CRABTREEBOOKS.COM

Title-Specific Learning Objectives:

Readers will:

- Explain that objects are made from materials that have properties.
- Understand that a material's properties make it useful for certain jobs or functions.
- Identify the reasons an author gives to explain why certain materials work for certain jobs or functions.

High-frequency words (grade one)	Academic vocabulary
a, all, an, are, be, can, is, our, the, there, this	fabric, functions, glass, materials, metal, object, plastic, properties, wood

Before, During, and After Reading Prompts:

Activate Prior Knowledge and Make Predictions:

Have children look at the images on the cover and on the title page. Encourage them to share answers to the following questions:

- What materials do you see?
- Choose one material. What does it look like? What does it feel like? Which words would you use to tell someone about it? What job does it do?

During Reading:

After reading pages 18 and 19, ask children to consider the reasons the author gives to prove that plastic is a good material for certain functions. Ask:

- Why is plastic a good material for the outside of a helmet? What other materials do helmets have?
- Why are objects for children often made with plastic?

After Reading:

Create a class T-Chart, or invite children to create their own T-Charts. Label the left column "object" and the right column "properties." Find objects and write them on the chart. Identify the properties of the object's materials on the side. As an extension, include a third column for children to write down why the material is a good fit for the object's use.

Author: Crystal Sikkens

Series Development: Reagan Miller

Editor: Janine Deschenes

Proofreader: Melissa Boyce

STEAM Notes for Educators: Janine Deschenes

Guided Reading Leveling: Publishing Solutions Group

Cover, Interior Design, and Prepress: Samara Parent

Photo research: Crystal Sikkens and Samara Parent

Production coordinator: Katherine Berti

Photographs:
iStock: nortonrsx: cover (bl); Kraig Scarbinsky: p. 12

All other photographs by Shutterstock

Library and Archives Canada Cataloguing in Publication

Title: The right material for the job / Crystal Sikkens.
Names: Sikkens, Crystal, author.
Description: Series statement: Full STEAM ahead! | Include index.
Identifiers: Canadiana (print) 20190133864 |
  Canadiana (ebook) 20190133872 |
  ISBN 9780778764397 (softcover) |
  ISBN 9780778763987 (hardcover) |
  ISBN 9781427123565 (HTML)
Subjects: LCSH: Materials—Juvenile literature.
Classification: LCC TA403.2 .S55 2019 | DDC j620.1/1—dc23

Library of Congress Cataloging-in-Publication Data

CIP available at the Library of Congress

LCCN: 2019023724

Printed in the U.S.A./102019/CG20190809

Table of Contents

Crabtree Publishing Company
www.crabtreebooks.com   1-800-387-7650

Published in Canada
Crabtree Publishing
616 Welland Ave.
St. Catharines, Ontario
L2M 5V6

Published in the United States
Crabtree Publishing
PMB 59051
350 Fifth Avenue, 59th Floor
New York, New York 10118

Published in the United Kingdom
Crabtree Publishing
Maritime House
Basin Road North, Hove
BN41 1WR

Published in Australia
Crabtree Publishing
Unit 3 – 5 Currumbin Court
Capalaba
QLD 4157

What are Objects?

Objects are all around us. An object is anything you can see and touch. A table is an object. A spoon is an object.

A swing is an object. Even your clothes are objects.

Objects are made of **materials**. There are many different kinds of materials. Some materials are wood, **plastic**, and **metal**.

metal

wood

plastic

Made of Materials

Objects can be made from one or more materials.

This umbrella is made of plastic, metal, and **fabric**.

fabric

metal

plastic

These balls are made of plastic.

Did you know the same object could be made from different materials?

These pictures both show plates, but one is made from paper and the other is made from glass. Can you think of a third material from which a plate could be made?

Properties of Materials

All materials have **properties**. Properties are used to describe the material. This means they tell us what the material is like.

wood

Some properties of wood are that it is hard, strong, and the color brown.

glass

One property of glass is that it is see-through.

rubber

Waterproof is a property of rubber. Waterproof materials keep water out.

Finding Properties

We can find out a material's properties in different ways. One way is by using our **senses**.

We have five senses. They are touch, taste, smell, sight, and hearing.

sight

hearing

smell

taste

touch

Our sense of touch lets us know if a material is smooth or rough. Our sense of sight helps us see a material's color.

sense of touch

sense of sight

The Right Material

Most objects are used for certain jobs or have certain **functions**. Objects are made from materials with properties that will help them work as they should.

A sponge is used to wash things. So it is made from materials that soak up water.

Life jackets keep us from sinking in water. They are made from materials that float.

Swimsuits are made from materials that dry quickly.

Using Fabric

Fabric is a material with different properties. Fabric can be used to make clothing.

There are many kinds of fabrics.

Some fabrics are thin and allow air to flow through them.

Summer clothes are made with thin fabrics to keep us cool.

Different Fabrics

Winter clothing is often made using thick, heavy fabrics. They keep us warm.

Choosing clothes with the right fabrics helps keep us safe in different weather. It would be dangerous to wear light clothing in cold weather!

Backpacks are made of strong fabric. They can hold many objects without tearing.

Plastic Objects

Can you guess what material is light, but hard to break? If you guessed plastic, you are right!

Plastic is used on bike helmets to **protect** our heads. It is light for us to wear, but hard to break if we fall.

Many objects for children are made of plastic. They are light to carry, but won't break if dropped.

These children are playing with plastic blocks. They are light and hard. The children can pick them up and click them together. If they are dropped, they do not break!

The Right Choice

Choosing the right material for an object is important. For example, houses need to give people shelter. So they are made from strong materials, such as bricks.

What would happen if fabric was used to make a table?

What material are windows made from?
Why is this material the right choice?

Would glass be a good idea to use when making clothes?
Why or why not?

Words to Know

fabric [FAB-rik] noun A cloth made by knitting or sewing together threads

function [FUHNGK-shuhn] noun The activity for which a thing is used

material [muh-TEER-ee-uhl] noun Thing from which something is made

metal [MET-l] noun A material cut from the earth

plastic [PLAS-tik] noun A human-made material. It can have many shapes and colors.

property [PROP-er-tee] noun A quality used to describe something

protect [pruh-TEKT] verb To keep from being hurt

senses [sens-is] noun The ways that the body helps us understand the world around us, including sight, sound, hearing, taste, and touch

A noun is a person, place, or thing.

A verb is an action word that tells you what someone or something does.

An adjective is a word that tells you what something is like.

Index

About the Author

Crystal Sikkens has been writing, editing, and providing photo research for Crabtree Publishing since 2001. She has helped produce hundreds of titles in various subjects. She most recently wrote two books for the popular Be An Engineer series.

To explore and learn more, enter the code at the Crabtree Plus website below.

www.crabtreeplus.com/fullsteamahead

Your code is:
fsa20

STEAM Notes for Educators

Full STEAM Ahead is a literacy series that helps readers build vocabulary, fluency, and comprehension while learning about big ideas in STEAM subjects. *The Right Material for the Job* uses strong examples to help readers identify the reasons an author gives to support points. The STEAM activity below helps readers extend the ideas in the book to build their skills in science, language arts, and engineering.

Which Materials Work Best?

Children will be able to:
- Use adjectives learned in the book to describe the properties of materials and connect the adjectives with the material's function.
- Create a plan for a structure with materials with properties that suit its purpose.

Materials
- Building with Materials Worksheet

Guiding Prompts
After reading *The Right Material for the Job*, ask children:
- What are properties? Can you think of some examples of properties from the book?
- Why are a material's properties important? How do they relate to the job or function of an object? Go through some examples with children, such as: Why are stop signs red?

Activity Prompts
Have children go on a "materials treasure hunt" in the class and share the materials they found. Ask them to describe the materials' properties. Refer to the properties in the book, such as:
- Hard, strong, see-through, waterproof, a certain color, soaks up or floats on water, thin, light, thick, heavy, hard to break, dries quickly.

Tell children that they need to create a structure that uses materials with appropriate properties. Give children options for their structure, or have all children create the same structure. For example, they can create a doghouse with strong materials on the outside and soft, warm ones on the inside.

Hand children the Building with Materials Worksheet. Have them draw a model of their structure and plan out its materials. They should use the word bank to fill in words that describe their chosen materials, and use the sentence frames to explain why they chose the materials they did. Discuss answers as a class.

Extensions
- Have children build simple structures with materials that suit a purpose. For example, have them create a wall of a certain height or a tool that will help keep their desk clean. Provide simple materials and time to plan. Discuss why chosen materials worked well.

To view and download the worksheets, visit **www.crabtreebooks.com/resources/printables** or **www.crabtreeplus.com/fullsteamahead** and enter the code **fsa20**.